I0821408

DRAMA

Essential Literary Genres

BY REBECCA KRAFT RECTOR

Essential Library

An Imprint of Abdo Publishing | abdopublishing.com

ABDOPUBLISHING.COM

Published by Abdo Publishing, a division of ABDO, PO Box 398166, Minneapolis, Minnesota 55439.

Printed in the United States of America, North Mankato, Minnesota
092016
012017

Interior Photos: GeorgiosArt/iStockphoto, 10–11; Mirrorpix/Newscom, 14; Lebrecht Music and Arts Photo Library/Alamy, 16, 21; Geraint Lewis/Alamy, 22–23, 28; The Print Collector/Heritage Images/Glow Images, 33; Everett Historical/Shutterstock Images, 35; Photofest, 37, 39, 43, 44–45; United Artists/Photofest, 54–55, 57, 60, 63; AP Images, 65, 73, 79; Herbert K. White/AP Images, 66–67; Columbia Pictures/Photofest, 83, 92–93; ABC/Photofest, 84; Joan Marcus/Photofest, 89; Universal Studios/Photofest, 91

Editor: Nick Rebman
Series Designer: Maggie Villaume

PUBLISHER'S CATALOGING-IN-PUBLICATION DATA

Names: Rector, Rebecca Kraft, author.
Title: Drama / by Rebecca Kraft Rector.
Description: Minneapolis, MN : Abdo Publishing, 2017. | Series: Essential literary genres | Includes bibliographical references and index.
Identifiers: LCCN 2016945202 | ISBN 9781680783780 (lib. bdg.) | ISBN 9781680797312 (ebook)
Subjects: LCSH: Literature--Juvenile literature. | Literary form--Juvenile literature.
Classification: DDC 809--dc23
LC record available at http://lccn.loc.gov/2016945202

CONTENTS

1

INTRODUCTION TO LITERARY GENRES

Why do we read and write literature? Telling stories is an integral part of being human, a universal experience across history and cultures. Literature as we know it today is the written form of these stories and ideas. Writing allows authors to take their readers on a journey that crosses the boundaries of space and time. Literature allows us to understand the experiences of others and express experiences of our own.

What Is a Genre?

A genre is a specific category, or type, of literature. Broad genres of literature include nonfiction, poetry, drama, and fiction. Smaller groupings include subject-based genres such as mystery, science fiction, romance, or fantasy. Literature can also be classified by its audience, such as young adult (YA) or children's, or its format, such as a graphic novel or picture book.

What Are Literary Theory and Criticism?

Literary theory gives us tools to help decode a text. On one level, we can examine the words and phrases the author uses so we can interpret or debate his or her message. We can ask questions about how the book's structure creates an effect on the reader, and whether this is the effect the author intended. We can analyze symbolism or themes in a work. We can dive deeper by asking how a work either supports or challenges society and its values or traditions.

You can look at these questions using different criticisms, or schools of thought. Each type of criticism asks you to look at the work from a different perspective. Perhaps you want to examine what the work says about the writer's life or the time period in which the work was created. Biographical or historical criticism considers these questions. Or perhaps you are interested in what the work says about the role of women or the structure of society. Feminist or Marxist theories seek to answer those types of questions.

How Do You Apply Literary Criticism?

You write an analysis when you use a literary or critical approach to examine and question a work. The theory you choose is a lens through which you can view the work, or a springboard for asking questions about the work. Applying a theory helps you think critically. You are free to question the work and make an assertion about it. If you choose to examine a work using racial criticism, for example, you may ask questions about how the work challenges or upholds racial structures in society. Or you may ask how a character's race affects his or her identity or development throughout the work.

Forming a Thesis

Form your questions and find answers in the work or other related materials. Then you can create a thesis. The thesis is the key point in your analysis. It is your argument about the work based on the school of thought you are using. For example, if you want to approach a work using feminist criticism, you could write the following thesis: The character of Margy in Sissy Johnson's *Margy Sings the Blues* uses her songwriting to subvert traditional gender roles.

HOW TO MAKE A THESIS STATEMENT

In an analysis, a thesis statement typically appears at the end of the introductory paragraph. It is usually only one sentence long and states the author's main idea.

Providing Evidence

Once you have formed a thesis, you must provide evidence to support it. Evidence will usually take the form of examples and quotations from the work itself, often including dialogue from a character. You may wish to address what others have written about the work. Quotes from these individuals may help support your claim. If you find any quotes or examples that contradict your thesis, you will need to create an argument against them. For instance: Many critics claim Margy's actions uphold traditional gender roles, even if her songs went against them. However, the novel's resolution proves Margy had the power to change society through her music.

HOW TO SUPPORT A THESIS STATEMENT

An analysis should include several arguments that support the thesis's claim. An argument is one or two sentences long and is supported by evidence from the work being discussed. Organize the arguments into paragraphs. These paragraphs make up the body of the analysis.

Concluding the Essay

After you have written several arguments and included evidence to support them, finish the essay with a conclusion. The conclusion restates the ideas from the thesis and summarizes some of the main points from the essay. The conclusion's final thought often considers additional implications for the essay or gives the reader something to ponder further.

HOW TO CONCLUDE AN ESSAY

Begin your conclusion with a recap of the thesis and a brief summary of the most important or strongest arguments. Leave readers with a final thought that puts the essay in a larger context or considers its wider implications.

In This Book

In this book, you will read summaries of works, each followed by an analysis. Critical thinking sections will give you a chance to consider other theses and questions about the work. Did you agree with the author's analysis? What other questions are raised by the thesis and its arguments? You can also see other directions the author could have pursued to analyze the work. Then, in the Analyze It section in the final pages of this book, you will have an opportunity to create your own analysis paper.

Drama

Dramas, also known as plays, are meant to be performed on a stage by a cast of actors who play the parts of the characters. The first dramas were probably performed by early people during religious ceremonies or festivals. Later, the ancient Greeks and Romans performed both tragedies and comedies, often in poetic form. Greek theater influenced Western drama, which typically tells stories through dialogue. Asian drama tends to use formal music, dance, and body movements to tell classical tales. Asian cultures do not have a tradition of tragic drama.

Dramas are written by playwrights in a specific format called a script, which tells the story through dialogue and stage directions. The dialogue may be written in the form of poetry or in the natural language of the time. Sometimes dialogue is meant to be sung. The actors use movement, as well as speech, to convey a sense of character. Stage directions are instructions that tell when actors enter and exit the stage, what the characters look like and what costumes they wear, what scenery is needed, and how the stage should be lit.

LOOK FOR THE GUIDES

Throughout the chapters that analyze the works, thesis statements have been highlighted. The box next to the thesis helps explain what questions are being raised about the work. Supporting arguments have also been highlighted. The boxes next to the arguments help explain how these points support the thesis. The conclusions are also accompanied by explanatory boxes. Look for these guides throughout each analysis.

2

AN OVERVIEW OF *SHE STOOPS TO CONQUER*

She Stoops to Conquer is a five-act play by Oliver Goldsmith. The play opened in London, England, in 1773 and was immediately successful. Goldsmith wanted to write a play that made people laugh, which was unusual for the time. The story concerns two gentlemen who go to the countryside and become entangled in a series of mistaken identities.

The play opens with a prologue in which an actor declares comedy is dying but Goldsmith (a medical doctor, as well as the

In addition to writing plays, Oliver Goldsmith was a successful novelist and poet.

play's author) might save it. The prologue is attributed to David Garrick, a popular actor of the time.

Tony Plays a Trick

Act One takes place in the home of Mr. and Mrs. Hardcastle. Mrs. Hardcastle expresses sadness over the fact that their old mansion looks like an inn. Mr. Hardcastle says he likes things that are old.

The couple discusses Tony Lumpkin, Mrs. Hardcastle's son by her first marriage. Tony is not yet 21 years old and therefore is not in control of his fortune. He enjoys practical jokes and lives at home. Tony comes on stage, and Mrs. Hardcastle tries to keep him from going to the alehouse. But Tony says he is stronger than she is and drags her offstage.

Mr. Hardcastle's daughter, Kate, joins her father and reminds him of their bargain: she may dress fashionably in the morning to visit with her friends, and in the evening she will put on the plainer clothing that he prefers her to wear. Mr. Hardcastle tells her that he has chosen the son of his friend to be her husband. The young man, Charles Marlow, is said to be sensible and good-natured but also bashful and reserved. Marlow is to arrive from London that evening.

Kate later tells her cousin, Constance Neville, about Marlow. Constance says Marlow is the best friend of George Hastings, Constance's admirer. She has heard that Marlow may be shy around upper-class women but is very different with lower-class women. They discuss Mrs. Hardcastle's efforts to marry Constance to her son, Tony, and how pleased they are that Tony has no desire to marry Constance. They know Mrs. Hardcastle only wants Constance's fortune in jewels, which Mrs. Hardcastle, as her guardian, controls until Constance marries.

Meanwhile, Hastings and Marlow stop at the alehouse to ask for directions to Hardcastle's house. Tony plays a joke, telling them it is a long, dangerous way. He suggests they stay the night at the inn down the road. Tony continues his trick by giving them directions to Hardcastle's house; he says the innkeeper will try to act like a gentleman.

Marlow's Misunderstanding

Act Two takes place at Hardcastle's house. Mr. Hardcastle is offended by the way he is treated by Marlow and Hastings, who think he is an innkeeper. Hardcastle tries to tell them stories, but they interrupt and ignore him. They demand to see the menu for tonight's supper and discuss what they should wear. Hardcastle thinks they're rude, but since they are his guests he tries to help them.

Hardcastle and Marlow leave to view the bedrooms. Constance comes into the room, and Hastings says he never expected to see her at an inn. She sets him straight, realizing that Tony must have tricked them. They discuss their plans to run away together, but Constance says she won't leave without her jewels.

Tony is a prankster, and his joke on Hastings and Marlow sets the play's events in motion.

Hastings says they must not tell Marlow that the house is not an inn because he will instantly want to leave. They need more time to convince Mrs. Hardcastle to give Constance her jewels.

Marlow joins them, and Hastings says Constance and Kate stopped at the inn after dining in the neighborhood. Marlow suggests he wait until tomorrow to see Kate, saying he dreads to meet her. Kate comes in and tries to engage him in polite conversation, but Marlow refuses to look at her and can barely speak to her. After they part, Kate decides he needs to be taught to be more confident. Later, Hastings and Tony talk, and Tony agrees to help Hastings and Constance with their elopement so his mother will stop trying to make Tony marry Constance.

Marlow Falls for a Barmaid

In Act Three, Kate dresses plainly to please her father. Mr. Hardcastle and Kate share their impressions of Marlow. Constance believes him to be awkwardly shy, while her father says he is rude. They agree he is not a good match for Kate, although she says if Marlow can show her some of the boldness her father has seen, she will like him better.

Marlow bows to Constance because she is an upper-class woman.

Tony steals Constance's jewels from his mother and gives them to Hastings. Constance is unaware of this and continues to argue with her aunt about wearing the jewels. Tony tells his mother to say the jewels have been stolen so Constance will stop arguing, and his mother does so. Constance is horrified until Tony tells her he has the jewels. Mrs. Hardcastle discovers the jewels really are missing, but Tony pretends to think her hysterics are meant to convince Constance.

Kate tells her maid that she is going to pretend to be a barmaid to fool Marlow. Kate wants to see how Marlow acts with lower-class women. When Marlow comes in, Kate asks if he needs anything. He is preparing to leave the inn but changes his mind when he sees how pretty she is. He never looked Kate in the face before, so he does not recognize her. He tries to kiss her, but she fends him off. Marlow quickly leaves when Mr. Hardcastle comes in and sees him trying to kiss Kate. Kate tries to convince her father that Marlow isn't really a scoundrel, but Mr. Hardcastle doesn't believe it.

Embarrassment for Marlow

In Act Four, Constance tells Hastings that Marlow's father will arrive soon. Marlow's father knows Hastings and can spoil their plans, so they must run away now. Hastings says he gave the jewels to Marlow for safekeeping. Later, Marlow tells Hastings he is attracted to the barmaid and that he gave the jewels to the landlady (Mrs. Hardcastle) for safekeeping. Hastings tells him not to seduce the barmaid but doesn't say Marlow has ruined his plans. Hastings decides he and Constance will have to elope without the jewels.

Hardcastle tells Marlow that Marlow's servants are getting drunk. Marlow, who still thinks he's at an inn, says it's good for the inn's business. Furious, Mr. Hardcastle tells Marlow to leave. Marlow demands his bill, and Mr. Hardcastle says Marlow's father made him expect a better young man.

Mr. Hardcastle storms out, and Marlow wonders if he's made a mistake. He asks Kate about the house and learns it is Mr. Hardcastle's home. Kate also says she is a poor relative of Mr. Hardcastle. Marlow is embarrassed; he must leave at once. Kate pretends to cry at the idea that he is leaving because she did something wrong. Marlow says Kate is the only one he leaves with reluctance. He says the difference in their stations makes a marriage impossible, though if he were to follow his desires he'd stay with her. Kate thinks he's admirable and decides to tell her father everything.

Knowing that Mrs. Hardcastle will give them the jewels if she thinks they are to be married, Tony and Constance pretend to love each other. Mrs. Hardcastle says she will give them the jewels and that they will marry the next day. Hastings sends Tony a letter asking him to bring a pair of fresh horses to the bottom of the garden where he is waiting to elope with Constance. Unfortunately Tony cannot read, and he asks his mother to read the letter for him. Constance tries to intercept the letter but fails. Mrs. Hardcastle is furious and says she will take Constance to her other aunt immediately, with Tony to guard them along the way.

After Mrs. Hardcastle leaves, Hastings and Marlow enter the room, angry at Tony and at each other. Tony says he will be a friend and that Hastings should meet him in two hours at the bottom of the garden.

Marlow Learns the Truth

In Act Five, Marlow's father, Sir Charles Marlow, has arrived. He and Mr. Hardcastle laugh at young Marlow's mistakes. They want their children to marry each other, and Mr. Hardcastle tells of seeing Marlow holding Kate's hand. Marlow joins the men and apologizes for his conduct. He assures them that nothing has happened between him and Kate. After he leaves, Marlow's father believes him to be sincere, but Hardcastle does not. Kate joins the two older gentlemen and says Marlow has told her he loves her. Sir Charles does not believe his shy son would say that, but the fathers agree to hide behind a screen in half an hour so they can hear for themselves.

Meanwhile, Tony has taken his mother in a closed carriage. Mrs. Hardcastle believes she is far from home, but Tony has actually taken her in circles. However, he has gotten the carriage stuck at the bottom of the garden. Tony tells Hastings, who is waiting there, to leave with Constance while he distracts Mrs. Hardcastle. Tony tells his mother they are far from home in a place full of thieves. They see a man coming, and Tony hides his mother behind a tree while he goes to meet the man, who is actually Mr. Hardcastle. Convinced the man is going to kill Tony, Mrs. Hardcastle runs out to beg for his life. Baffled, Mr. Hardcastle explains where she is, and Mrs. Hardcastle realizes what Tony has done.

Constance refuses to run away with Hastings after all, saying they will need her fortune. She wants to wait and ask Mr. Hardcastle to mediate for them with his wife. Reluctantly, Hastings agrees.

Meanwhile, Marlow says good-bye to Kate, and Mr. Hardcastle joins Sir Charles behind the screen. Marlow says he will stay and that his father will approve. Kate, still pretending to be a poor relative, says she will not marry him when their stations in life are so different. Marlow gets onto his knees, and his father bursts out, saying Marlow deceived him by claiming he was indifferent to Kate. Marlow is confused until Mr. Hardcastle says Kate is his daughter. Marlow is again embarrassed and says he must leave, but Mr. Hardcastle says his daughter will forgive him.

Marlow's father and Mr. Hardcastle hide behind a screen as Marlow and Kate say good-bye.

Mrs. Hardcastle and Tony come in, saying Constance has run off with Hastings. But Mrs. Hardcastle says she doesn't care since she still has the jewels. Mr. Hardcastle reminds her that if Tony refuses to marry Constance when he is of age, Constance will be in control of her own fortune. Hastings and Constance return, and Hardcastle asks Tony if he refuses Constance's hand in marriage. Hardcastle reveals that Tony is already 21 years old. Tony quickly refuses Constance, saying she may marry whom she pleases. Marlow congratulates Hastings and Constance, and he wishes Kate will forgive him. Hastings urges Kate to have Marlow. Kate's father joins their hands and says Kate will have him.

3

RETHINKING SOCIAL CLASS

Social class refers to a person's status or place in society. In the 1770s, when *She Stoops to Conquer* was written, society was clearly divided between the rich upper classes and the poor lower classes. Rules of society dictated the attitudes of the social classes as well as how the classes treated each other.

When performing a social class analysis of drama, differences between the portrayals of classes as a whole can be examined. Such an analysis could compare and contrast characteristics between the rich and the poor, such as food, clothing, shelter, and

Mr. Hardcastle, *left,* experiences frustration when Marlow, *right,* mistakenly believes Hardcastle belongs to a lower social class.

occupations. Another way to analyze social class would be to look at the way the characters are treated because of their social class.

The play *She Stoops to Conquer* portrays a range of social classes. The play revolves around the mistakes made when the visiting gentlemen are unaware of everyone's true social class. The mistakes are set in motion by a country gentleman, Tony, who cares nothing for social class distinctions and enjoys drinking with farm laborers at the alehouse. In contrast, social class distinctions mean everything to Marlow, the visiting gentleman from the city. Social status forms the basis for his behavior, and he views everyone through the lens of social class. He acts differently with people from different classes, and his mistakes arise from this behavior. Marlow believes social class is an indicator of a person's worth, and he treats people accordingly until he is shown that worth is not dictated by social status.

THESIS STATEMENT

The thesis statement in this analysis states: "Marlow believes social class is an indicator of a person's worth, and he treats people accordingly until he is shown that worth is not dictated by social status." This thesis answers the question: How does social class affect the way characters in the play are treated?

Marlow speaks and acts freely with women of a lower class because he thinks he is better than they are, but he is unable to speak to higher-class women because he thinks they are above him. He believes he is better than a barmaid and therefore finds it easy to be himself. He says, "I'm doomed to adore the sex, and yet to converse with the only part of it I despise."[1] His friend Hastings says Marlow is an idiot with upper-class women. Marlow explains that upper-class women are a more tremendous object than a comet and they petrify him. Hastings advises him to say even half of the fine things he says to lower-class women, but Marlow says a single glance from a gentlewoman is too much for him.

ARGUMENT ONE

The first argument of the thesis states: "Marlow speaks and acts freely with women of a lower class because he thinks he is better than they are, but he is unable to speak to higher-class women because he thinks they are above him." The author argues that Marlow's behavior toward women is dictated by his view of their social status.

Marlow treats Mr. Hardcastle poorly when he believes he is an innkeeper

ARGUMENT TWO

The second point of the essay states: "Marlow treats Mr. Hardcastle poorly when he believes he is an innkeeper but is respectful and apologetic when he learns he is a gentleman." The author supports this argument with examples of how Marlow treats Mr. Hardcastle.

but is respectful and apologetic when he learns he is a gentleman. Marlow greets Mr. Hardcastle "with a loud voice, a lordly air, and a familiarity that made my blood freeze."[2] Mr. Hardcastle is confused by these actions because Marlow's father said he was modest. Marlow tells Mr. Hardcastle to see that his boots are taken care of, demands to see a menu, and examines the bedrooms. Mr. Hardcastle sees Marlow as a bully and soon tries to kick him out of his house. When Marlow is told who Mr. Hardcastle is, he is mortified. "To mistake this house of all others for an inn, and my father's old friend for an innkeeper! What a swaggering puppy must he take me for! What a silly puppy do I find myself!"[3] Marlow begins to see that his perceptions may not always be correct, saying, "I can scarce reflect on my insolence without confusion."[4]

ARGUMENT THREE

The third point of the essay states: "Marlow treats Kate differently when she is an upper-class woman, a barmaid, and a poor relative; eventually he learns that her worth is not determined by status." The author is now proving the final point of the thesis with evidence showing how Marlow treats Kate differently according to her status, while Kate herself does not change.

Marlow treats Kate differently when she is an upper-class woman, a barmaid, and a poor relative; eventually he learns that her worth is not determined by status.

The three faces of Kate demonstrate the way Marlow treats the different classes. When Kate first appears as an upper-class woman, Marlow tries to escape meeting with her and begs that Hastings not leave him alone with her. He treats Kate with respect but stutters and can't look at her. Constance tells Kate this is how Marlow treats all upper-class women. Kate decides to "stoop to conquer" and takes on the manners of a barmaid to see how he will behave. With the barmaid, Marlow is bold, complimentary, and daring in his actions. He tries to kiss Kate and, rather than tell her his real name, gives her a false name. Then Kate says she is a poor relative—someone much higher in status than a barmaid but not someone who possesses wealth. Marlow does not treat poor relatives the same way he treats barmaids. He apologizes for his prior behavior, saying his "stupidity saw everything the wrong way."[5] When he thinks Kate is a poor member of an upper-class family, he acknowledges his attraction to her but says he cannot marry her because of the difference in their stations. However, the rules of society finally loosen their grip on Marlow, and he tells Kate, "I can have no happiness but what's in your power to grant me!"[6]

Kate, *right*, assumes a range of social classes over the course of the play.

Throughout the play, Marlow is condescending to the lower classes, saving his politeness and consideration for those he believes are equal to him. By the end of the play, Kate has shown him that the gentlewoman, barmaid, and poor relative are the same person—and her worth did not change according to her station. Marlow falls in love with the poor relative and finally realizes he can find value in people despite their apparent social class.

CONCLUSION

This final paragraph is the conclusion. It sums up the author's arguments and partially restates the original thesis, which has now been backed up with evidence.

THINKING CRITICALLY

Now it is your turn to assess the critique. Consider these questions.

1. The thesis argues that Marlow treats people differently according to their social class. Do you agree? Why or why not?
2. What was the strongest argument? What was the weakest? Did the evidence support the arguments?
3. Do you agree with the conclusion? Could other arguments have been made to support the thesis and reach the conclusion?

OTHER APPROACHES

What you have just read is one possible way to apply social class criticism to the play *She Stoops to Conquer*. What are some other ways to approach it? Keep in mind that analyzing a work using a social class analysis can mean examining not only the portrayal of the social classes but also how this affects the characters' behavior. Following are two alternate approaches.

Truth Seekers

Tony Lumpkin and Kate Hardcastle both dress and act in ways that are not typical of their social class. Tony wears common clothing, frequents a tavern, and does not want to live a life concerned with social status. Kate dresses plainly to please her father and later does so to discover the truth of Marlow's personality. A social class analysis exploring these issues might have the following thesis statement: Both Tony Lumpkin and Kate Hardcastle discard the conventions of their social class to seek a life based on truth.

Social Class as Comedy

The comedy of the play hinges on actions based on assumptions of social class standing. There would be no humor if the characters and audience did not believe that people act in certain ways because of their social status. Because Tony appears to be a simple, poorly dressed inhabitant of the tavern, he is able to mislead Marlow and Hastings into thinking Mr. Hardcastle's home is an inn. This leads to more humor as the gentlemen become embroiled in misunderstandings. Kate's disguises as women of different classes lead to further humorous situations. A social class analysis examining this idea might have the following thesis statement: Overturning society's strict etiquette concerning class distinctions is the driving force behind the play's humor.

AN OVERVIEW OF *PYGMALION*

Pygmalion was written by George Bernard Shaw and first produced in Vienna, Austria, in 1913. In the play, Henry Higgins wagers that he can teach the lower-class Eliza Doolittle to speak and act like a duchess. The title comes from the myth of the sculptor Pygmalion, who falls in love with his statue of the perfect woman.

The Notetaker

The five-act play is set in Victorian England. Act One opens in Covent Garden. Most of the characters are not named in this act. They are simply referred to with descriptions such as the mother, the flower girl, and the bystander. A mother is with her adult son and daughter. She orders her son, Freddy, to get them a cab. As Freddy leaves, he bumps into a young woman selling flowers,

George Bernard Shaw was notorious for his controversial political views.

who tells him in a thick accent to watch where he's going. Freddy apologizes as he rushes away.

A bystander tells the flower girl that a gentleman is writing down everything she says. The flower girl and the bystander think the notetaker is a detective and that she is in trouble. However, the man reveals he is a researcher of phonetics—the way language is spoken. He says he could even pass off the flower girl as a duchess at an ambassador's garden party. Another gentleman introduces himself as Colonel Pickering, a student of Indian dialects. The notetaker identifies himself as Henry Higgins and says he was planning to go to India to meet Pickering. They agree to go to Pickering's motel for supper. Freddy returns with a taxi, but his mother and sister have left. The flower girl grandly announces that she will take a taxi home.

The Wager

Act Two is set in the house of Henry Higgins, where Higgins has been showing Pickering his research. The housekeeper, Mrs. Pearce, announces that a young woman is here to see Higgins. The flower girl from the night before, Eliza Doolittle, says she has come to take lessons to learn how to speak better. "I want to be

Although Eliza, *left*, is uneducated at the beginning of the play, she is intelligent and independent.

a lady in a flower shop stead of selling at the corner of Tottenham Court Road. But they won't take me unless I can talk more genteel," she says.[1]

Pickering wagers that Higgins cannot pass her off as a lady at the ambassador's garden party in six months. Mrs. Pearce protests, but Higgins agrees to the challenge. He is rude to Eliza, saying she has no feelings worth considering. Higgins stops her from leaving by saying, "If you are not found out, you shall have a present of seven-and-sixpence to start life with as a lady in a shop."[2] Mrs. Pearce takes Eliza away for a bath and orders new clothes for her. Pickering says he feels responsible for Eliza and that Higgins must not take advantage of her. Higgins says, "What! That thing!"[3]

Eliza's father, Alfred Doolittle, arrives. He was told that Eliza asked her landlord to send all her possessions to Higgins's house. Doolittle says he wants his daughter back, although he actually wants money. Higgins gives Doolittle five pounds. As Doolittle is leaving, he doesn't recognize Eliza, who is clean and dressed in a kimono. Mrs. Pearce tells Eliza that her new clothes have arrived, and Eliza howls in excitement and rushes off. Pickering and Higgins agree they have a difficult task ahead of them.

The Visitors

Act Three takes place in Higgins's mother's house, some months after Eliza began her lessons. Higgins enters his mother's drawing room and explains his experiment with Eliza. Mrs. Higgins is not pleased, but Higgins says he has taught her to speak properly and that her orders are to speak of only the weather and everybody's health. He admits Eliza's pronunciation is fine, but what she pronounces may not be.

Visitors arrive. They are Mrs. Eynsford-Hill and her daughter Clara, the same mother and daughter from

In the film adaptation of the play, Eliza uses a candle to practice her accent; the flame wavers when she pronounces H-sounds correctly.

Act One. Soon Freddy and Colonel Pickering follow. Eliza arrives and impresses everyone with her grace and beauty. Her speech is formal and precise until Mrs. Eynsford-Hill mentions influenza. Eliza, still speaking with precise and correct vowels, announces that her aunt died of influenza and it is Eliza's belief "they done the old woman in."[4] The others are surprised, and Higgins quickly says it is the "new small talk."[5]

When Eliza is ready to leave, Freddy offers to walk with her. She says, "Walk! Not bloody likely. I am going in a taxi."[6] The older people are shocked at her use of the curse word "bloody," but Clara is impressed and imitates her.

Once everyone has left, Mrs. Higgins scolds her son and Pickering, asking what will happen to Eliza when their experiment is over. The men assure her that Eliza is quick and is learning everything very well.

The Argument

Act Four takes place in Higgins's house immediately after the ambassador's party. Although the party is not shown, it is obvious Eliza was successful. Higgins, Pickering, and Eliza come in, all dressed in evening clothes. The men ignore Eliza and check the mail. Higgins wonders where his slippers are. Eliza leaves and returns with them. Pickering congratulates Higgins on winning his bet, and they comment on how glad they are that it is over.

Pickering, who moved in to help with Eliza's instruction, goes up to bed. Higgins follows, telling Eliza to put out the lights and let Mrs. Pearce know he wants tea at breakfast. Eliza is furious. When Higgins returns, looking for his slippers, she throws them at him. She says she won his bet for him but that she doesn't matter any more than his slippers.

Higgins says, "YOU won my bet! You! Presumptuous insect! I won it."[7] He goes on to say he doesn't know what is to become of her—she can get married, or Pickering could set her up in a flower shop. Eliza asks if her clothes belong to her, since she doesn't want to be accused of stealing when she leaves. She even returns a ring he bought for her. Higgins throws it at the fire, saying, "You have wounded me to the heart."[8] After Higgins leaves, Eliza looks for the ring.

The Departure

Act Five opens in Mrs. Higgins's house, where Higgins and Pickering burst in with the news that Eliza is gone.

Eliza succeeds in playing the role of a duchess.

Mrs. Higgins is appalled to learn they've asked the police to look for Eliza as if she is a possession of theirs. Pickering does not believe the police will look for her, since they suspect Higgins "of some improper purpose."[9]

Mr. Doolittle enters the room, dressed in fashionable clothes. He reveals that Higgins wrote a letter to an American millionaire, mentioning "that the most original moralist at present in England . . . was Alfred Doolittle, a common dustman."[10] The millionaire died and left Doolittle money with the condition that he lecture for the millionaire's pet project—a society to reform the morals of society. Apparently the millionaire did not understand that Higgins was joking and that Doolittle actually had few morals. Doolittle says he doesn't mind the lecturing, but he doesn't want to be a gentleman, and now all his relatives want money from him. Mrs. Higgins says this solves the problem of what is to become of Eliza; now her father can provide for her. Higgins says that's nonsense—Doolittle has no right to take Eliza since he already took five pounds for her.

Mrs. Higgins reveals that Eliza is upstairs and came to her because of the brutal way Higgins and Pickering treated her. The men protest, but Mrs. Higgins says Eliza worked hard for them and they didn't even thank her. Higgins is impatient with the idea, but Pickering admits they may have been inconsiderate. Mrs. Higgins says Eliza will not return to Higgins's house, but "she is quite willing to meet you on friendly terms and to let bygones be bygones."[11] Higgins reluctantly agrees to behave himself, and Eliza is sent for. Mr. Doolittle waits on the balcony so Eliza won't have to deal with his news before she makes up with Higgins and Pickering.

Eliza comes in and greets Higgins and Pickering politely. Higgins is furious, saying, "Get up and come home; and don't be a fool."[12] He goes on to say he "created this thing out of the squashed cabbage leaves of Covent Garden."[13] Eliza ignores him and thanks Pickering for treating her like a lady and teaching her manners. Pickering says Higgins taught her to speak. She responds, "You see, really and truly, apart from the things anyone can pick up (the dressing and the proper way of speaking, and so on), the difference between a lady and a flower girl is not how she behaves, but how she's treated."[14] Pickering always treats her like a lady and Higgins like a flower girl. Pickering asks her to forgive Higgins and return with them. Higgins says, "Forgive! Will she, by George! Let her go. Let her find out how she can get on without us."[15]

Mr. Doolittle explains he's headed for the church to get married and hopes Eliza will come. Pickering urges Eliza to go, and she agrees. Pickering and Mrs. Higgins ask if they may come as well, and Doolittle says he'd be honored. Mrs. Higgins exits to get ready, and Pickering leaves with Doolittle, again asking Eliza to forgive Higgins and to come back to stay with them.

Eliza and Higgins are left alone. Higgins rants that he treats everyone the same—that he could do without her but will miss her. Eliza says Higgins always tries to get everyone to do what he wants but doesn't really care for anybody. They argue, and Eliza reveals that Freddy has been writing to her and is in love with her. Freddy will be kind to her and not bully her. Higgins continues to rant and call her an idiot, and Eliza says, "I can't talk to you: you turn everything against me: I'm always in the wrong. But you know very well all the time that you're nothing but a bully."[16] She says she will marry Freddy or teach phonetics.

Mrs. Higgins returns to say the carriage is waiting. Eliza says good-bye to Higgins, saying she will not see him again. Higgins tells Eliza to order a ham and cheese for him and to buy him gloves and a tie. She tells him to buy them himself and leaves. Mrs. Higgins tells him

In 1956, *Pygmalion* was adapted into a successful musical called *My Fair Lady*.

she'll buy him the tie and gloves. Higgins says "sunnily" that Eliza will buy them for him. The stage directions say he "disports himself in a highly self-satisfied manner."[17]

That is the original ending. Shaw revised the play several times over the years, and a later version has a slightly different ending. After Higgins gives orders to Eliza about things to buy, she corrects him. She tells him what size gloves he would need if he wanted them lined with lamb's wool, that Colonel Pickering prefers a different cheese, and that she already reminded Mrs. Pearce about the ham. Before she sweeps out she says, "What you are to do without me, I cannot imagine."[18] Higgins tells his mother that Eliza is going to marry Freddy and roars with laughter.

5

A SURPRISING CHANGE

Analyzing drama from a feminist point of view means examining the portrayal of women, especially compared with the portrayal of men. The analysis focuses on women's actions, speech, opportunities, and power. Are these equal to those of men? Or are the women in an inferior position and portrayed as weak individuals without intelligent minds or needs of their own? Are the women viewed as objects and evaluated based on appearance? Stereotypical antifeminist roles depict women solely as daughters, mothers, caregivers, or obedient wives.

Eliza's job as a flower seller leads other characters to treat her as an object rather than a person with independent thoughts.

In *Pygmalion*, Henry Higgins makes a wager with Colonel Pickering that Higgins can teach flower girl Eliza Doolittle how to speak and act like a lady. In addition, he says that after six months he will be able to pass her off as a duchess at the ambassador's garden party. The play is set in Victorian England, where people are born into a certain social class distinguished by money, speech, and education. Women are expected to be obedient daughters, wives, and mothers, whose aim is to please the dominant male. The wealthy and privileged Higgins and Pickering do not doubt that they can treat the lowly Eliza in any way they please. Higgins does not know it, but the subject of his experiment will surprise him. The uneducated Eliza is an intelligent and independent woman whom Higgins treats as an object, but she still manages to grow into a strong, confident woman with a mind of her own.

Eliza demonstrates her intelligence and independence even when

THESIS STATEMENT

The thesis statement in this analysis states: "The uneducated Eliza is an intelligent and independent woman whom Higgins treats as an object, but she still manages to grow into a strong, confident woman with a mind of her own." This thesis answers the question: How is the main female character portrayed in the play?

she is an uneducated flower seller. She has left her father's home and is supporting herself. She knows her rights when she thinks a policeman is going to arrest her, saying, "I've a right to sell flowers if I keep off the kerb."[1] She's shrewd about people, demanding to see what Higgins has written about her. "How do I know whether you took me down right? You just shew me what you've wrote about me," she says.[2]

ARGUMENT ONE

The first argument of the thesis states: "Eliza demonstrates her intelligence and independence even when she is an uneducated flower seller." The author argues that Eliza was already a strong female before she met Higgins.

Eliza looks to the future rather than trying to survive day to day. She sells flowers on the street corner, but she has a goal of being a lady in a flower shop. She knows she needs to speak better and makes the decision to pay Higgins for lessons. She stands up for herself against Higgins when he makes rude comments, saying, "Well, I ain't come here to ask for any compliment; and if my money's not good enough I can go elsewhere."[3] When Higgins agrees to the wager, Eliza says, "You're a great bully, you are. I won't stay here if I don't like. I won't let nobody wallop me."[4]

ARGUMENT TWO

The second point of the essay states: "Throughout the play, Higgins treats Eliza as an object to be shaped and 'created' into something new." The author supports this argument with examples of how Eliza is treated as an object.

Throughout the play, Higgins treats Eliza as an object to be shaped and "created" into something new. Higgins does not see Eliza as a person but only as the raw material from which he will mold his duchess. As the subject of a wager, Eliza is treated as if she has no feelings or identity of her own. Higgins says when they are finished with her, they "can throw her back into the gutter."[5]

Mrs. Higgins recognizes that her son and, to a lesser extent, Pickering are not viewing Eliza as a person with wants and needs of her own. She tries to make them see that they need to consider the consequences of their actions. When she fails, she calls them "a pretty pair of babies, playing with your live doll."[6]

Even when Eliza is learning everything Higgins teaches her, Higgins doesn't recognize her intelligence, merely likening her to a parrot. After the bet is won, both Pickering and Higgins congratulate themselves and don't realize Eliza's hard work enabled her to carry off the masquerade. When she argues with Higgins about it, he calls her a "presumptuous insect."[7] He even acts as if she is his possession, saying about her father, "She doesn't belong to him. I paid him five pounds for her."[8]

But Eliza grows into a woman who knows her own mind and is confident that she can move forward in life without Higgins. When she succeeds in her charade as a duchess, she tries to get Higgins to acknowledge and appreciate her. When he doesn't, she throws his slippers at him, saying, "I'd like to kill you, you selfish brute."[9] But then she realizes she controls her own destiny. Eliza has options; she can marry Freddy, open a flower shop, or teach phonetics. She tells Higgins, "Oh, when I think of myself crawling under your feet and being trampled on and called names, when all the time I had only to lift up my finger to be as good as you, I could just kick myself."[10] Higgins tries to convince her to stay, saying she will fall back into the gutter without him. However, Eliza has grown, while Higgins has stayed the same. He continues to view her the way he always has. He says, "If you come back I shall

ARGUMENT THREE

The third point of the essay states: "But Eliza grows into a woman who knows her own mind and is confident that she can move forward in life without Higgins." The author is now proving the final point of the thesis with evidence that shows Eliza's confidence in herself.

treat you just as I have always treated you. I can't change my nature; and I don't intend to change my manners."[11]

Eliza finally sees Higgins for the man he is—and even though she may have feelings for him, she realizes he will never see her as his equal or as the intelligent woman she is. She is decisive about parting with him, firmly telling him she will not see him again. When he ignores this and tells her to take care of some errands for him, including buying him gloves and a tie, she disdainfully says, "Buy them yourself" and, according to the stage directions, "sweeps out."[12]

Despite Higgins's best efforts to treat Eliza as a "cabbage leaf" that he has turned into a lady, she proves to be intelligent and independent. With her new skills, she is confident she can move forward in life. She does not need to put up with bullying. She is not a passive female, subservient to Higgins's supposed superior maleness. She is a worthy person in her own right.

CONCLUSION

This final paragraph is the conclusion of the essay. The author's arguments are summarized, and the thesis is partially restated. Evidence has been presented to support the thesis.

THINKING CRITICALLY

Now it is your turn to assess the critique. Consider these questions.

1. The thesis argues that Eliza was intelligent and independent before she met Higgins and grew into a stronger, more confident woman afterwards. Do you agree? Why or why not?
2. Did the author use the strongest arguments to support the thesis? What other arguments and evidence could have been presented?
3. Is the conclusion effective in summarizing the arguments and supporting the thesis? What changes would you make?

OTHER APPROACHES

What you have just read is one possible way to apply feminist criticism to the play *Pygmalion*. What are some other ways to approach it? Keep in mind that analyzing a work using feminist criticism means examining the portrayal of women, especially in comparison to the portrayal of men. Following are two alternate approaches.

Eliza versus Higgins

Throughout most of the play, Eliza allows herself to be used and manipulated by Higgins. She does not rebel when he treats her poorly, and she performs traditional female tasks for Higgins such as keeping track of his slippers, performing his errands, and conveying his demands to the housekeeper. He constantly needles her until she stands up for herself at the end of the play. Some literary critics say Eliza could never have grown as a woman if Higgins had not constantly treated her poorly. A feminist analysis examining these ideas might have the following thesis statement: Higgins's self-centered belief in his own superiority and his subsequent poor treatment of Eliza provide a testing ground in which Eliza's generous and independent spirit is honed to its full maturity.

Strong Women, Weak Men

Examining gender roles in the play, it can be said that most of the men act selfishly, while most of the women see the broader picture and consider others in their decisions. Higgins frequently acts childishly, and his mother and the housekeeper try to make him act like an adult. Freddy is ordered about by his mother and sister. A feminist analysis of this aspect of the play might have the following thesis statement: In contrast to the play's Victorian setting, with its patriarchal view of men as strong and wise, the major women characters in the play act with wisdom and compassion, while the men are portrayed as weak and childish.

6

AN OVERVIEW OF *INHERIT THE WIND*

Inherit the Wind is a three-act play written by Jerome Lawrence and Robert E. Lee. It was first performed in 1955. The plot was inspired by the 1925 Scopes "monkey" trial and, similar to the historical event, concerns a Tennessee teacher who is on trial for the crime of teaching Charles Darwin's theory of evolution. The title of the play comes from the Bible: "He that troubleth his own house shall inherit the wind."[1]

Brady's Arrival

The script of the play includes a preface in which the authors say the play is not history

The people of Hillsboro create numerous signs displaying their religious beliefs.

or journalism but theater. Act One takes place in July in the small town of Hillsboro, Tennessee. Rachel Brown, the 22-year-old daughter of the town's minister, visits her boyfriend and fellow teacher, Bert Cates. Bert is awaiting trial for teaching Darwin's theory of evolution. Rachel urges Bert to say it was all a joke, but he refuses. She reminds him that it's a crime to teach evolution in Tennessee, and everyone thinks he was wrong to do it. He admits he broke the law but says he wasn't necessarily wrong. After Rachel leaves, Bert and the bailiff talk about the famous Matthew Harrison Brady, who will be prosecuting the case. Bert says a Baltimore newspaper is sending someone to defend him, but he doesn't know who it will be.

A crowd is waiting to welcome Mr. and Mrs. Brady. People have erected stands selling hot dogs, lemonade, fans, and Bibles. At the instigation of Reverend Jeremiah Brown, men hang a banner that says Read Your Bible so Brady will know it is a religious town. E. K. Hornbeck, a journalist from the *Baltimore Herald*, makes cynical comments. Townspeople sing hymns and carry antievolution banners as they welcome Brady. The mayor asks Brady to give a speech. Brady says he has come not only to prosecute Bert but also to defend the scripture.

The mayor declares Brady an honorary colonel in the state militia.

At a lunch in Mr. Brady's honor, Mrs. Brady reminds her husband that the doctor told him not to overeat. But he consumes huge portions of potato salad and chicken. Brady learns that Rachel knows Bert, and he speaks with her away from everyone else. Their talk is not heard by the audience. The reporter, Hornbeck, reveals that his newspaper is sending the famous Henry Drummond to defend Bert. Reverend Brown says Drummond is an ungodly man and that they will not let him into town. But Brady says they should welcome him because

Hornbeck shakes hands with an ape as a resident of Hillsboro gives a speech about the theory of evolution.

a victory over someone as prominent as Drummond will impress the world. Brady says he will easily defeat Drummond because of what Rachel has told him.

Rachel runs to the courthouse to talk to Bert. Hornbeck follows and shows her an article he wrote, portraying Bert favorably. Rachel wishes the townspeople could read it, but she doesn't see how Bert can be right if the great Brady is against him.

Jury Selection

A few days later, the courtroom is packed as Brady and Drummond choose jurors from the local people. Ten jurors have already been picked. Brady approves the eleventh juror when he says he attends church. Drummond approves him when he says he is illiterate and has never read the Bible or Darwin. Brady approves the twelfth man when he says he believes in God and in Brady. Drummond says this juror is not acceptable and dismisses him.

When the judge refers to the prosecutor as Colonel Brady, Drummond objects. He says it prejudices the case against his client. Therefore, the mayor makes Drummond a temporary colonel. The twelfth juror is chosen when he says his wife tends to religious matters for both of them, and he just works at the feed store.

Brady accuses Drummond of trying to trick and confuse the men they are choosing for the jury. But Drummond says he's trying to defend the Constitution. The judge says court is recessed until tomorrow and announces that the Reverend Brown is having a prayer meeting. Drummond objects, saying the Read Your Bible banner should be removed—or another should be put up saying Read Your Darwin. The judge says that's preposterous. Most people leave, stopping to congratulate Brady on their way out.

Rachel pleads with Drummond to call off the trial. Drummond says he'll stop the trial if Bert really thinks he did wrong, but Bert says he won't quit. Bert asks Rachel to support him, but she says Brady will be calling her to the stand to testify against him. Bert says if she repeats the personal things he said to her, the town will "crucify" him.[2] Rachel admits to Drummond that she's confused and afraid of her father.

Prayer Meeting

Act Two takes place at the prayer meeting on the courthouse lawn. Reverend Brown works the crowd into a frenzy, asking them if they cast out the sinner in their midst. The crowd shouts yes, and Brown prays for God to strike down Bert. Rachel protests, and the reverend prays that the same punishment be brought against his daughter, Rachel. Brady interrupts, saying that perhaps Brown is overzealous. Brady reminds Brown that God forgives his children. Brady sends everyone home but stops Drummond to remind him that they used to be friends and respected each other. He wonders why Drummond has moved away from him. Drummond

Rachel, *second from left*, and Bert, *third from left*, sit nervously in the courtroom.

replies, “All motion is relative. Perhaps it is you who have moved away—by standing still.”[3]

The Trial

Two days later, in the courtroom, Brady makes a speech against evolutionists. The audience applauds. Drummond calls Howard, one of Bert’s students, to the stand. Drummond asks Howard what he thinks of Darwin’s theory, saying he’s trying to show that Howard has the right to think. Brady objects, and the judge agrees that the right to think is not on trial. Drummond insists it is, but he is overruled. Next, Drummond asks Howard if evolution harmed him, and Brady objects again. Finally, Drummond asks if Howard believes the theory of evolution. Howard says he’s not sure and needs to think about it. Drummond says the Bible doesn’t mention things such as telephones and asks whether those things are therefore evil. Brady and Drummond discuss the concept of morality, and Drummond says truth is more important as a direction.

Brady calls Rachel to the stand, where she explains that Bert stopped going to church after the reverend said a drowned boy was writhing in hell because he’d never been baptized. Bert yells that religion should comfort people. Brady pushes Rachel to talk more about Bert's religious views and twists the things she tells him. She almost has a breakdown on the stand and is dismissed. Brady rests his case.

Drummond calls three scientists to the stand to testify about evolution, but the judge does not allow it. Drummond calls Brady to the stand to testify about the Bible, and Brady agrees to testify. Under questioning, Brady says he has memorized a large part of the Bible but has never read Darwin. Brady says every word in the Bible should be taken literally.

Drummond asks why God gave man the power to think if he wasn't supposed to use it. They argue over the age of a rock; scientists say it is millions of years old, which Drummond says proves the Bible can't be taken literally. The crowd begins to grow excited, and Brady says Drummond is trying to destroy people's belief in the Bible. Drummond responds that he's "trying to stop you bigots and ignoramuses from controlling the education of the United States!"[4]

Brady says God speaks to him, and he knows that God didn't speak to Darwin because God told him so. Drummond mocks him, calling him a prophet and the mouthpiece of God. The crowd laughs, and Brady breaks

Brady, *standing*, speaks to the court as Drummond looks on.

down, raving about the Bible. The judge adjourns the court while Mrs. Brady comforts her husband.

The Verdict

In Act Three, everyone is waiting for the jury's verdict. Drummond tells Bert about Golden Dancer, a rocking horse that was beautiful in the store window but broke when he tried to ride it. He wants Bert to keep searching for the truth of things.

The mayor tells the judge the people at the capitol are worried about the press coverage and says the judge should go easy on Bert if he's declared guilty. The jury declares Bert guilty, and Bert gives a statement saying he's only a teacher but believes he's being "convicted of violating an unjust law" that he will continue to fight.[5] A woman calls out that he's not a teacher anymore.

The judge fines Bert $100 and sets bail at $500. Brady demands a harsher penalty, but the judge simply says Drummond may appeal the case in a higher court. Brady wants to read some remarks, but the judge declares the court adjourned and tells Brady to read them to the crowd. The crowd babbles and shouts across the courtroom, and vendors begin selling their goods. No one pays attention to Brady except the reporter, who asks him to move closer to the radio microphone. But then the reporter says they're out of time. Brady suddenly collapses and is carried out of the courtroom, reciting the inauguration speech of a new president.

Bert asks Drummond if he won or lost. Drummond says he won because people will read in the paper that he "smashed a bad law."[6] Bert prepares to go to jail until he can pay his bail, but he discovers that the *Baltimore Herald* has put up the money. Rachel comes in with a suitcase and says she's leaving her father. She gives Bert his copy of Darwin, saying she's read it and didn't understand it but she's no longer afraid to think.

The courtroom was packed at the 1925 Scopes trial.

The judge returns and announces that Brady is dead. Hornbeck says it was from a "busted belly."[7] Hornbeck then makes a sarcastic comment about Brady and his religion. Drummond is furious, saying there was greatness in the man. Drummond quotes the Bible and says perhaps Brady was looking for God in the wrong place. Hornbeck accuses him of being a hypocrite, saying Drummond is just as religious as Brady.

Hornbeck leaves to type up his story. Bert and Rachel decide to leave town on the same train as Drummond. Drummond picks up the Bible and the book by Darwin and balances them in each hand. He puts them together and shoves them into his briefcase, side by side, and then crosses the empty square.

7

HISTORICAL LINKS

A historical analysis of a drama considers the events and culture of the time period in which the play was written. The analysis may also consider events mentioned in the play itself. The historical analyst must research the playwright's contemporary world to recognize significant influences on the work. An analysis may examine the influence of the time period on the play's plot, characters, and setting. Aspects of historical influences or portrayals can be examined for such details as accuracy, exaggeration, and purpose. The research may also bring to light deeper meanings or alternative views of the play's significance.

Joseph McCarthy contributed to a fear of communism that came to be known as the Red Scare.

The plot of *Inherit the Wind* has its roots in the 1925 trial of teacher John Scopes, who was accused of teaching Darwin's theory of evolution, which was a crime at that time in Tennessee. The playwrights studied transcripts and used many elements of the trial in their story. An examination of the time period in which the play was written reveals that in the 1950s, US Senator Joseph R. McCarthy was a prominent figure. McCarthy said hundreds of Communists had infiltrated the government, and he tried to uncover hidden Communists throughout the country. Some saw McCarthy as a defender of American beliefs, while others considered him an enemy to American personal freedoms. Playwrights Lawrence and Lee wrote *Inherit the Wind* knowing the Scopes trial would be a good vehicle for exploring the issues of their own times. Although it was based on a 1920s historical event, the play was fictionalized in such a way as to enhance parallels to 1950s society's fears over the McCarthy–era "witch hunts."

THESIS STATEMENT

The thesis statement in this analysis states: "Although it was based on a 1920s historical event, the play was fictionalized in such a way as to enhance parallels to 1950s society's fears over the McCarthy–era 'witch hunts.'" This thesis answers the question: How do historical events affect the portrayal of events in the play?

The playwrights referred to transcripts and newspaper accounts of the actual trial, but they did not write the play as a true representation of the historical event; they imply the play has a broader significance that surpasses the boundaries of time and place. In an introduction, the playwrights emphasize the play is "not history" and it "does not pretend to be journalism."[1] They go on to say, about the original lawyers Williams Jennings Bryan and Clarence Darrow, "the issues of their conflict have acquired new dimension and meaning in the thirty years since they clashed."[2]

ARGUMENT ONE

The first point of the essay states: "The playwrights referred to transcripts and newspaper accounts of the actual trial, but they did not write the play as a true representation of the historical event; they imply the play has a broader significance that surpasses the boundaries of time and place." The author argues that the play has a greater meaning than a simple representation of history.

The play is not set in 1928, the time of the historical trial. Instead, "It might have been yesterday. It could be tomorrow."[3] The play's defense lawyer, Drummond, emphasizes this point when he's talking to Bert, the accused, after the trial. Even though Bert is declared guilty, Drummond says it's a victory because people will read in the newspapers that he stood up against a bad law. Drummond goes on to say, "You don't suppose this kind of thing is ever finished, do you? Tomorrow it'll be something else—and another fella will have to stand up."[4]

ARGUMENT TWO

The second point of the essay states: "Exaggerations for dramatic effect also made stronger parallels to McCarthy-era issues." The author supports this argument with examples that show how exaggerations echoed McCarthy-era issues and events.

Exaggerations for dramatic effect also made stronger parallels to McCarthy-era issues. Many of the real-life events and people were changed, magnified, or made more extreme in the play. This made the play more exciting, but it also allowed audiences of the 1950s to recognize and relate the play to their current events. During the Scopes trial, in the real town of Dayton, Tennessee, the townspeople were welcoming and hospitable—even to Clarence Darrow, the attorney defending the teacher. In the play, however, the people of Hillsboro are hostile, prejudiced, and talk about striking down and casting out "the sinner." This echoes the "witch trial" feel of the McCarthy era. In reality, John Scopes was well liked, never went to jail, and was allowed to keep his job, although he decided to go to graduate school rather than continue teaching.

In the play, the teacher is locked up, the townspeople despise him, and he loses his job. Bert says, "People look at me as if I was a murderer. Worse than a murderer!"[5] This echoes the intolerance shown by McCarthy and his followers. McCarthy blacklisted people he thought were Communists; although he never provided any proof, the people were then ostracized, and many lost their jobs. At the Scopes trial, the prosecutor was courteous to witnesses. In the play, Brady is mostly rabid and intolerant. This echoes McCarthy's own manner toward those he accused.

The play's arguments for intellectual freedom could be applied equally well to those who were Communists as to those who supported evolution. Drummond, the play's defense attorney, presents arguments that go beyond the controversy of evolution versus religion. He says, "An idea is a greater monument than a cathedral."[6] Drummond argues for the right to think and the right to be wrong. He also argues

ARGUMENT THREE

The third point of the essay states: "The play's arguments for intellectual freedom could be applied equally well to those who were Communists as to those who supported evolution." The author is now proving the final point of the thesis with evidence that shows how the intellectual freedom arguments could be applied to the events of the playwright's time period.

that truth is more important than the moral values of what is good and bad. He says, "But one of the peculiar imbecilities of our time is the grid of morality we have placed on human behavior: so that every act of man must be measured against an arbitrary latitude of right and longitude of wrong—in exact minutes, seconds, and degrees!"[7]

At the end of the play, Rachel emphasizes the point by the change in her attitude to new ideas, as well as ideas contrary to her religious beliefs: "You see, I haven't really thought very much. I was always afraid of what I might think—so it seemed safer not to think at all. But now I know. A thought is like a child inside our body. It has to be born. If it dies inside you, part of you dies, too!"[8]

Inherit the Wind enjoyed an enormous success, perhaps as a result of its dramatization of the intellectual controversy and fears that were rampant in its contemporary society. The fictional town's anger and turmoil about an individual with different beliefs paralleled 1950s society's questions about intellectual freedom and McCarthy's hunt for Communists. The ideas presented in the play could be discussed in the context of contemporary life, as the audience explored

Clarence Darrow, *left*, and William Jennings Bryan speak during the 1925 Scopes trial.

CONCLUSION

This final paragraph is the conclusion. In the conclusion, the author sums up the arguments and partially restates the original thesis, which has now been backed up with evidence from the text. The author also presents a new idea, that the play's success may be attributed to the parallels between the play and contemporary issues.

parallels between the Hillsboro fundamentalists' and McCarthy supporters' attacks on intellectuals.

THINKING CRITICALLY

Now it is your turn to assess the critique. Consider these questions.

1. The thesis argues the play is based on a historical event but is dramatized so parallels with the McCarthy era were enhanced. Do you agree? Why or why not?
2. The arguments were supported by both textual evidence and historical evidence. Was this an effective technique in supporting the arguments? Can you think of other textual or historical evidence that would have been more effective?
3. A conclusion may introduce a new, related idea. Do you think this conclusion did that effectively? What was the new idea? What other ideas might have been stronger?

OTHER APPROACHES

What you have just read is one possible way to apply historical criticism to the play *Inherit the Wind*. What are some other ways to approach it? Keep in mind that analyzing a work using a historical analysis means examining the events and culture existing at the time the work was written, as well as the portrayal of events in the play itself. Following are two alternate approaches.

Science and Society

Society in the 1920s was changing rapidly, with new scientific ideas and advances in technology and communication. For instance, the Scopes trial was the first to be shared on a radio broadcast. A historical analysis examining this idea might have the following thesis statement: The play dramatizes the effect of new scientific ideas and advances in 1920s society.

City versus Country

With urbanization and immigration on the rise in the early 1900s, city people generally were exposed to new ideas more than country dwellers, who tended to stay in one place and to be more conservative in their thinking. A historical analysis examining this contrast might have the following thesis statement: The play explores the clash of different mindsets between country and city dwellers.

8

OVERVIEWS OF *A RAISIN IN THE SUN AND MAMMA MIA!*

A Raisin in the Sun was written by Lorraine Hansberry and premiered in New York City in 1959. It is the story of the Youngers, a poor African-American family that has different ideas on how to spend an insurance check. The three-act play takes place on the South Side of Chicago in the late 1940s or early 1950s.

Act One opens in the crowded three-room apartment of the Younger family, where Ruth awakens her son, Travis, and her husband, Walter. Travis sleepily gathers his clothes and heads out of the apartment to the shared hall bathroom. Walter asks if the check is coming today even though it's not due until the next day.

Playwright Lorraine Hansberry was only 28 years old when *A Raisin in the Sun* premiered.

According to the stage directions, Walter always speaks with a "quality of indictment," or accusation, in his voice.[1] He tells Ruth he wants to open a liquor store with two other men, but she isn't supportive. His sister Beneatha comes in from the bedroom she shares with their mother. Beneatha is a college student who wants to be a doctor. When Walter mentions the check, Beneatha says the insurance money from their father's death belongs to their mother Lena, who is known as Mama. Walter is furious and says Beneatha should be like other women and be a nurse or just get married.

After Walter storms out, Mama comes out of her bedroom and checks on a little plant on the windowsill. Ruth says Mama, Ruth's mother-in-law, should give Walter some of the money so he can be happy, but Mama is against selling liquor. She says Ruth looks tired and should stay home from her housecleaning job, but Ruth refuses. When Ruth asks what Mama is going to do with the money, she says some of it will go to Beneatha's education. She's also thinking of making a down payment on a house with a yard for Travis. Mama and her late husband, Big Walter, had always dreamed of having a house. Mama goes on to talk about Big Walter and how he loved his children. Beneatha joins them, and they discuss her rich boyfriend, George Murchison. Beneatha says she doesn't intend to marry him. Mama and Beneatha then fight about God. After Beneatha leaves, Ruth passes out on the floor.

The next day, Walter goes to meet the men about the liquor store. No one knows where Ruth has gone, but Mama suspects she went to the doctor. Beneatha invites her African friend, Joseph Asagai, to the apartment. Ruth returns to say she is two months pregnant. Mama is suspicious when Ruth lets it slip that her doctor is a woman; their family doctor is a man.

Asagai brings Beneatha presents of Nigerian robes and music, and they talk about Africa. The $10,000 insurance check arrives, and Walter returns with the business papers for the liquor store. He wants to talk about the liquor store, but Ruth wants to tell him she's pregnant. Walter yells that no one listens to him, and Mama tells him again that she is not going to invest in a liquor store.

Walter angrily starts to leave, but Mama tells him Ruth is pregnant. Mama says she's worried that Ruth will have an abortion, but Walter doesn't believe it until Ruth opens the bedroom door to say she has already given the doctor a down payment. Mama tells Walter to act like his father and tell his wife not to have an abortion. Instead he walks out the door.

A New House

Act Two takes place in the apartment later the same day. Beneatha dances to Nigerian music, wearing the clothes that Asagai gave her. Walter comes home drunk and dances too. He fights with George, Beneatha's rich boyfriend, when George arrives for a date. Beneatha removes the Nigerian headdress and shows them she has cut her hair into an Afro. Everyone is shocked. After Beneatha and George leave, Ruth and Walter fight but make up. Mama says she has made a down payment on a house in a white neighborhood, which is worrisome to all of them because they will be the only black family. Mama says it was the best house they could afford and that there will be room for bunk beds in Travis's room. Ruth is happy about moving into a house, but Walter is angry and says Mama has butchered his dream.

A few weeks later, as the family packs for the move, their neighbor Mrs. Johnson visits. She tells them about a black family whose house in a white neighborhood was bombed. She thinks the same thing will happen to the Youngers. After she leaves, Walter's boss calls to tell Ruth that Walter hasn't shown up in three days and he'll be fired if he doesn't come in the next day. Walter doesn't care; he has been driving around and drinking. Mama blames herself for Walter's behavior and gives him the remaining insurance money. She put $3,500 down on the house, leaving $6,500. Mama says Walter should put $3,000 into a savings account for Beneatha's education, and the remaining $3,500 should go in a checking account with his name on it. Walter is ecstatic and tells his son he's going to make a business transaction that will change their lives.

Mama is extremely frustrated by Walter's behavior.

A week later, it's moving day. Everyone, even Walter, is happy. Mr. Lindner, a white man from their new housing development, visits and offers the Youngers money to not move into their new house. They kick him out. The doorbell rings, and Walter happily greets one of his business partners. But the man has come to say that Willy, the other partner, has run off with all their money. Mama asks whether Walter has also lost the money for Beneatha's education, and he admits he has. Mama says Big Walter worked himself to death for that money and that Walter just gave it away.

Mr. Lindner, *left*, offers the Younger family money to stay out of the neighborhood.

Walter's Decision

Act Three takes place an hour later, still in the apartment. Asagai comes to help with the packing, and Beneatha tells him what Walter has done. Asagai invites her to return to Africa with him, and she says she must think. Walter says he has called Lindner to come back so they can do business. Mama is upset, saying five generations of her family never took money to be told they were less than anyone else. Beneatha says Walter is no brother of hers, but Mama reminds her to love him despite everything he has done.

Lindner arrives, and Mama insists that Travis remain so he can understand what Walter is doing. With Travis watching, Walter changes his mind. He tells Lindner they don't want his money, they have worked hard to be able to move, and they have no plans to cause trouble in their new neighborhood. Lindner leaves, and the moving men arrive. Ruth and Mama share their pride in Walter, and they all leave the apartment, with Mama carrying her plant.

Mamma Mia!

Mamma Mia! is a two-act musical written by Catherine Johnson. Producer Judy Craymer asked Johnson to create a play around the songs of the musical group ABBA. *Mamma Mia!* premiered in London in 1999 and includes 25 ABBA songs. The play is about a girl who invites three strangers to her wedding in hopes that she will find her father among them.

Wedding Plans

The play starts with a prologue in the post office of a Greek island where 20-year-old Sophie mails wedding invitations to three men who may be her father—Sam, Bill, and Harry. Act One takes place three months later when two of Sophie's friends arrive for the wedding. Sophie confides that she found her mother's diary and invited her three possible fathers to her wedding. Raised by a single mother, Sophie hopes her father will walk her down the aisle. She has not told her mother. Sophie's mother, Donna, welcomes her own friends, Rosie and Tanya, to the island. The three women used to form a famous singing group, Donna and the Dynamos. Donna tells her friends about her money troubles running her taverna.

Later, the three men arrive at the taverna. They realize they were all on the island 21 years ago. Sophie greets them; she tells them Donna doesn't know about the invitations, and it will be a lovely surprise. Sam says it's a big mistake because Donna said she never wanted to see him again. Sophie convinces him to stay but doesn't tell them she suspects one of them is her father. Donna comes in and tries to send all of them away. They are determined to stay, however, and Donna leaves.

Donna's friends discuss men and marriage. Donna tells them Sophie's possible fathers are here. She feels they are ruining Sophie's wedding. She is not happy that Sophie is getting married, but she won't let the men spoil things. That night, Sophie's fiancé, Sky, goes to his bachelor party, and the women have a party for Sophie. Donna and the Dynamos sing for them. Sam, Harry, and Bill show up, and Sophie meets each of them alone. Sam asks Sophie why he's there, but she doesn't answer; she tells Harry she doesn't know who her dad is; Sophie tells Bill that Donna got the money to build the taverna from a Greek lady named Sophia. Bill says he had a Great Aunt Sophia, and he knows her money went to family. Bill says he may be her father. He agrees to give Sophie away tomorrow and to keep it a secret from Donna. Sam and Harry also agree to give her away because each thinks he is the father.

Wedding Interruption

In Act Two, Sophie has a nightmare, and Donna comes to check on her. Donna thinks Sophie is having second thoughts about the wedding and says she'll sort things out. Sophie says she loves Sky and won't let her kids grow up not knowing who their father is.

Later, Sam tells Donna she's living his dream in the taverna he designed. He offers to help by inspecting the roof. She refuses, saying running a taverna is a lot of hard work, and she's glad she doesn't have any middle-aged men around to bother her.

In the bar, Harry asks Tanya what the father of the bride usually does, and she says he pays for everything. One of Sky's friends tries to flirt with Tanya, but she says he's just a little boy.

On the beach, Sophie tells Sky she invited the three possible dads and now everything is a mess because she didn't know her father as soon as she saw him. Sky is angry because she kept a secret from him, and he believes she planned the wedding only so she could find her father. Sky says now he doesn't know if Sophie really wants to get married. Sam wanders by and says Sophie needs to be sure it's what she really wants. Sophie says it has nothing to do with Sam and that her mother is okay

Tanya, Donna, and Rosie, *left to right*, perform a song as Donna and the Dynamos.

with it. Sam says Donna doesn't know anything about marriage but he does, and it doesn't always turn out happily-ever-after. Sophie says she loves Sky and is sure it will be all right.

Harry gives Donna a generous check to cover the wedding. She tries to refuse it, but Harry says he knows it must have been difficult to raise Sophie on her own. Donna helps Sophie get ready for the wedding, and Sophie says her friends think Donna is "so cool" for being a single mom and running her own business.[2] Donna says she had no choice since her mother disowned her. Sophie becomes emotional and asks her mother to give her away.

At the beach, Sam tells Donna that Sophie wants her father at the wedding and that her father wants to be there too. He wants to talk about his relationship with Donna, but Donna doesn't want to hear it.

Bill tells Rosie he is Sophie's dad, and he's confused because Sophie changed her mind about him giving her away. He didn't want to walk down the aisle anyway because he's a lone wolf. Rosie urges him to consider her as a girlfriend, and they kiss.

In the chapel, Donna interrupts the wedding to tell Sophie that her dad is present, and Sophie says she knows. Donna says she doesn't know which of them it is. When Sam gets upset, Donna says it's his fault since he left her to go back to his fiancée. He says he left to break off his engagement, but when he came back Donna was off with someone else. So he went home and married his fiancée. Harry speaks up to say it would be great to have even a third of Sophie—there are all kinds of families, and his is with his boyfriend, Lawrence. Sam and Bill agree that being a third of Sophie's dad is great. Sophie doesn't know which one is her dad but says she doesn't mind. She calls off the wedding and tells Sky

Donna and Sam struggle with their past relationship but come together at the end of the play.

they'll leave the island and tour the world. Sam says not to waste a good wedding and asks Donna to marry him. He's divorced, so Donna admits she loves him. In an epilogue, Sky and Sophie say good-bye to the others as they leave for the mainland.

9

THE IMPACT OF POWER DYNAMICS ON FAMILIES

A family analysis of a drama examines the portrayal of a family in the play. The analysis can examine both psychological and sociological aspects of the portrayal, and the family may be considered as a whole, as individual members, or both. When a family analysis is performed on two plays, aspects of the families are compared and contrasted.

Some aspects that may be considered include the values and beliefs of the family, roles within the family, and how family members react to crisis. Other questions

Walter tries to live up to Mama's expectation that he be more like his late father.

may include who holds the power, whether the history of the family influences today's members, and what the communication patterns are in the family.

In *A Raisin in the Sun,* an African-American family is being torn apart by money problems and individual differences. The play includes social commentary on African-American life in the mid-1900s, including issues of racial and sexual prejudice. In contrast to *A Raisin in the Sun*'s serious tone and claustrophobic apartment setting, *Mamma Mia!* is cheerful and takes place on beaches and in a taverna. *Mamma Mia!* deals with single motherhood and unknown paternity, but the tone stays lighthearted. Despite their differences, both *A Raisin in the Sun* and *Mamma Mia!* are portraits of families impacted by change. The dynamics of power are an important influence on the changing families in both plays.

THESIS STATEMENT

The thesis statement in this analysis states: "The dynamics of power are an important influence on the changing families in both plays." This thesis answers the question: How do the dynamics of power impact the changing families in the plays?

Absent fathers are a powerful force in both plays. In *A Raisin in the Sun*, Mama often talks about her late husband, Big Walter. Mama frequently says she expects her son to live up to Big Walter's good qualities, especially his love for his family. Big Walter's death casts the family into turmoil—over how to spend his insurance check, as well as the shifting dynamic of who is now the head of the household. The family members see the insurance check as a chance to follow their dreams: Mama to buy a house, Walter to invest in a business, and Beneatha to pursue her education. Mama expects Big Walter's influence to prevail. When Ruth talks about getting an abortion, Mama wants Walter to act like his father and show his love for his children and family. He does not. When Walter is planning to take the money offered by Lindner, Mama reminds him of how his father would have responded. When Mama forces Walter to speak in front of his son, Walter finally acts as she wishes—like Big Walter would act.

ARGUMENT ONE

The first point of the essay states: "Absent fathers are a powerful force in both plays." The author argues that the absence of the fathers in both families drives the action in both plays.

In *Mamma Mia!* Donna never speaks of Sophie's father. Sophie's desire to know who her father is causes her to send wedding invitations to three possible fathers. Sophie is sure she will recognize her father as soon as she sees him. But she has no idea which man is her father, and instead of happily preparing for her wedding, she is troubled and confused. Her mother won't talk about the past; Sophie says her mother doesn't understand that Sophie feels like her life has a big question that needs to be answered. This puts Donna and Sophie at cross-purposes and drives the action of the play.

ARGUMENT TWO

The second point of the essay states: "Power in each family is held by strong women who deal with change in different ways." The author supports this argument with examples of how both Mama and Donna deal with change.

Power in each family is held by strong women who deal with change in different ways. Both plays feature women who are single parents and unexpectedly come into money. They both use the money to create a home for their family. Mama buys a house, and Donna builds a taverna. After Big Walter's death, Mama tries to control the family by making all the important decisions. She tells everyone, especially her son, Walter, how to act, and she buys the family a house.

Donna is not a busybody like Mama, and she allows Sophie to make her own decisions. Donna thinks Sophie should not get married but does all she can to give her a successful wedding. When Sophie is upset before the wedding, Donna assumes she doesn't want to get married and says she'll fix it. However, when Sophie says she's in love and is going to get married, Donna allows the wedding to proceed. In the aftermath of Sophie's decision to invite the three men to the wedding, Donna exposes her own secrets and deals with her own issues; she allows the family to be redefined and expanded.

The plays offer very different views of a man's position in the family. Mama thinks a man should be the head of the family. She would like Walter to take on this role, but she doesn't trust him. Mama feels guilty when Walter says she has butchered his dream, so she gives him the rest of the insurance money and tells him to be the head of the family the way he is supposed to be. When Walter loses all their money, Mama still tells her daughter to support him and consider everything he's going through, even though Walter has lost the money that would pay for Beneatha's education.

ARGUMENT THREE

The third point of the essay states: "The plays offer very different views of a man's position in the family." The author is now proving the final point of the thesis with evidence that shows how men are viewed within the family structures and how this influences the ways the families handle change.

Donna is unmarried; she has no man and doesn't need one. When she became pregnant, she did not notify the possible fathers. She raised her daughter alone and runs the taverna to support them both. When the three men return to the island, she sees no place for them in her family or in her life. She tells them to go away and tries to keep the presence of her daughter secret. She says she is thankful every morning that she doesn't have a man around to bother her. Sophie's interference, though, forces her to deal with the fact that the men deserve a place in her family. Ultimately she welcomes them in, allowing all three men to claim a share in Sophie's paternity.

A Raisin in the Sun and *Mamma Mia!* are very different plays—one is serious and grim, while the other is a lighthearted musical—but both portray families in crisis. The dynamics of power, including absent fathers, strong women, and a man's role in the family, all influence how each family deals with challenges.

CONCLUSION

This final paragraph is the conclusion. The author restates the thesis in part and summarizes the supporting arguments. The thesis has been backed up with evidence that shows different power dynamics influenced how the families dealt with change.

THINKING CRITICALLY

Now it is your turn to assess the critique. Consider these questions.

1. The thesis argues that the dynamics of power are important in *A Raisin in the Sun* and *Mamma Mia!* Do you agree? Why or why not?
2. The author argues that the mothers in the plays hold power within the family. Do you agree? Who else holds power? Could an effective argument supporting the thesis be made about that person?
3. Mama believes a man should be the head of the household. Donna disagrees, saying she does not need a man in her life. With whom do you agree? Why?

OTHER APPROACHES

What you have just read is one possible way to apply a family analysis to the plays *A Raisin in the Sun* and *Mamma Mia!* What are some other ways to approach it? Keep in mind that a family analysis of a drama can examine both the psychological and sociological aspects of the portrayal of a family as a whole, or of its individual members. Following are two alternate approaches.

Dreams Deferred

Families in both plays have unfulfilled dreams. Some of the characters actively work toward their fulfillment, such as Mama and Walter. Others, such as Sophie, Sky, and Donna, have traded their old dreams for new ones. A family analysis examining this idea might have the following thesis statement: Both plays show families dealing with the question asked by Langston Hughes in his poem "Harlem"—"What happens to a dream deferred? / Does it dry up / like a raisin in the sun?"[1]

Families Betrayed

Betrayal is a factor that impacts both families. For example, Walter feels betrayed by his family, and he is actually betrayed by his business partner. Donna is betrayed by Sam and then by Sophie when Sophie invites the three possible fathers to the wedding. A family analysis that examines these issues might have the following thesis statement: Dealing with betrayal disturbs the balance of the families but ultimately makes them stronger.

ANALYZE IT!

Now that you have learned different approaches to analyzing a work, are you ready to perform your own analysis? You have read that this type of evaluation can help you look at literature in a new way and make you pay attention to certain issues you may not have otherwise recognized. So, why not use one of these approaches to consider a fresh take on your favorite work?

First, choose a philosophy, critical theory, or other approach and consider which work or works you want to analyze. Remember the approach you choose is a springboard for asking questions about the works.

Next, write a specific question that relates to your approach or philosophy. Then you can form your thesis, which should provide the answer to that question. Your thesis is the most important part of your analysis and offers an argument about the work, considering its characters, plot, or literary techniques, or what it says about society or the world. Recall that the thesis statement typically appears at the very end of the introductory paragraph of your essay. It is usually only one sentence long.

After you have written your thesis, find evidence to back it up. Good places to start are in the work itself or in journals or articles that discuss what other people have said about it. You may also want to read about the author or creator's life so you can get a sense of what factors may have affected the creative process. This can be especially useful if you are considering how the work connects to history or the author's intent.

You should also explore parts of the book that seem to disprove your thesis and create an argument against them. As you do this, you might want to address what others have written about the book. Their quotes may help support your claim.

Before you start analyzing a work, think about the different arguments made in this book. Reflect on how evidence supporting the thesis was presented. Did you find that some of the techniques used to back up the arguments were more convincing than others? Try these methods as you prove your thesis in your own analysis paper.

When you are finished writing your analysis, read it over carefully. Is your thesis statement understandable? Do the supporting arguments flow logically, with the topic of each paragraph clearly stated? Can you add any information that would present your readers with a stronger argument in favor of your thesis? Were you able to use quotes from the book, as well as from other critics, to enhance your ideas?

Did you see the work in a new light?

GLOSSARY

DEFER
To postpone or delay.

DUSTMAN
A garbage collector.

DYNAMICS
Motivations and driving forces.

MORALIST
A person with strong opinions about right and wrong.

OVERZEALOUS
Having too much enthusiasm, often for a belief or cause.

PLAYWRIGHT
A person who writes plays.

PREJUDICE
An unfair feeling of dislike for a person or group because of race, sex, or religion.

PRESUMPTUOUS
Bold and disrespectful.

PSYCHOLOGICAL

Relating to the mind and emotions.

SOCIOLOGICAL

Relating to social issues and behavior.

STAGE DIRECTION

An instruction to the actor or director that is written in the script of a play.

STEREOTYPICAL

Having to do with an often unfair and untrue belief that many people have about all people or things with a particular characteristic—for example, gender or race.

SUBSERVIENT

Very willing or too willing to obey someone else; less important than something or someone else.

TAVERNA

A Greek guesthouse with a bar.

THEORY OF EVOLUTION

A scientific explanation for the diversity of life on Earth; the diversity is caused by gradual changes to plants and animals over long periods of time.

WITCH HUNT

The act of searching out and punishing people who have unpopular opinions or views.

ADDITIONAL
RESOURCES

SELECTED BIBLIOGRAPHY

Andersson, Benny, Björn Ulvaeus, Judy Craymer, and Philip Dodd. *Mamma Mia! How Can I Resist You?: The Inside Story of Mamma Mia! and the Songs of ABBA.* London: Weidenfeld & Nicolson, 2006. Print.

Goldsmith, Oliver. *She Stoops to Conquer.* Ed. James Ogden. 2nd ed. London: Black, 2001. Print.

Hansberry, Lorraine. *A Raisin in the Sun*. New York: Vintage, 1994. Print.

Lawrence, Jerome, and Robert Edwin Lee. *Inherit the Wind.* New York: Ballantine, 2007. Print.

Shaw, Bernard. *Pygmalion: A Romance in Five Acts.* London: Penguin, 2003. Print.

FURTHER READINGS

Drama for Students: Presenting Analysis, Context and Criticism on Commonly Studied Dramas. Detroit: Gale Cengage, 2015. Print.

Elish, Dan. *Plays.* New York: Cavendish Benchmark, 2012. Print.

Grace, Fraser, and Clare Bayley. *Playwriting.* London: Bloomsbury, 2016. Print.

WEBSITES

To learn more about Essential Literary Genres, visit **booklinks.abdopublishing.com**. These links are routinely monitored and updated to provide the most current information available.

FOR MORE INFORMATION

For more information on this subject, contact or visit the following organizations:

Costume Museum at the Wick Theatre
7901 North Federal Highway
Boca Raton, FL 33487
561-995-2333
http://www.thewick.org/museum
The Costume Museum at the Wick Theatre features an exhibit of costumes from Broadway plays such as *My Fair Lady*, *Camelot*, and *Titanic*.

John F. Kennedy Center for the Performing Arts
VSA Playwright Discovery Award Program
2700 F Street, NW
Washington, DC 20566
800-444-1324
http://education.kennedy-center.org/education/vsa
The Kennedy Center is a premier performing arts center. The VSA Playwright Discovery Award Program encourages writers (with and without disabilities) in grades 6 to 12 to submit a one-act script of any genre about the disability experience. Free resources are available to help with the playwriting process.

Juilliard School
60 Lincoln Center Plaza
New York, NY 10023
212-799-5000
http://www.juilliard.edu/campus-life/library-archives
The Julliard School is not only a leading performance arts school with degree programs in acting and playwriting, but it also has an extensive resource collection, including rare manuscripts that may be viewed by appointment.

SOURCE NOTES

CHAPTER 1. INTRODUCTION TO LITERARY GENRES

None.

CHAPTER 2. AN OVERVIEW OF *SHE STOOPS TO CONQUER*

None.

CHAPTER 3. RETHINKING SOCIAL CLASS

1. Oliver Goldsmith. *She Stoops to Conquer*. Ed. James Ogden. 2nd ed. London: Black, 2001. Print. 29.
2. Ibid. 51.
3. Ibid. 71.
4. Ibid. 82.
5. Ibid. 71.
6. Ibid. 92.

CHAPTER 4. AN OVERVIEW OF *PYGMALION*

1. George Bernard Shaw. *Pygmalion and Major Barbara.* New York: Bantam, 1992. Print. 190.
2. Ibid. 215.
3. Ibid. 217.
4. Ibid. 244.
5. Ibid.
6. Ibid. 246.
7. Ibid. 259.
8. Ibid. 264.
9. Ibid. 267.
10. Ibid. 270.
11. Ibid. 275.
12. Ibid. 277.
13. Ibid. 278.
14. Ibid. 280.
15. Ibid. 281.
16. Ibid. 291
17. Ibid. 294
18. Bernard Shaw. *Pygmalion: A Romance in Five Acts*. London: Penguin, 2003. Print. 105.

CHAPTER 5. A SURPRISING CHANGE

1. George Bernard Shaw. *Pygmalion and Major Barbara*. New York: Bantam, 1992. Print. 190.

2. Ibid. 191.

3. Ibid. 204.

4. Ibid. 215.

5. Ibid. 213.

6. Ibid. 250.

7. Ibid. 259.

8. Ibid. 273.

9. Ibid. 259.

10. Ibid. 292.

11. Ibid. 284.

12. Ibid. 293.

CHAPTER 6. AN OVERVIEW OF *INHERIT THE WIND*

1. "Proverbs 11:29." *King James Bible Online*. King James Bible Online, n.d. Web. 14 July 2016.

2. Jerome Lawrence and Robert Edwin Lee. *Inherit the Wind*. New York: Ballantine, 2007. Print. 54.

3. Ibid. 67.

4. Ibid. 98.

5. Ibid. 115.

6. Ibid. 122.

7. Ibid. 125.

CHAPTER 7. HISTORICAL LINKS

1. Jerome Lawrence and Robert Edwin Lee. *Inherit the Wind*. New York: Ballantine, 2007. Print. 1.

2. Ibid. 1

3. Ibid. 1

4. Ibid. 123.

5. Ibid. 50.

6. Ibid. 93.

7. Ibid. 93.

8. Ibid. 124.

CHAPTER 8. OVERVIEWS OF *A RAISIN IN THE SUN* AND *MAMMA MIA!*

1. Lorraine Hansberry. *A Raisin in the Sun*. New York: Vintage, 1994. Print. 25.

CHAPTER 9. THE IMPACT OF POWER DYNAMICS ON FAMILIES

1. Langston Hughes. "Harlem." *Poetry Foundation*. Poetry Foundation, n.d. Web. 14 July 2016.

INDEX

ABOUT THE AUTHOR

Rebecca Kraft Rector is the author of *Early River Valley Civilizations* (Rosen, 2016), *Alan Turing* (Rosen, 2015), *Conrad to the Rescue* (Mondo, 2014), and *Tria and the Great Star Rescue* (Delacorte, 2002). She is a freelance writer, a former librarian, and a member of the Society of Children's Book Writers and Illustrators.